CALL 999!

SYLVIA MOODY

Illustrated by Toni Goffe

Oxford University Press 1995

Oxford University Press, Walton Street, Oxford OX2 6DP

Oxford New York
Athens Auckland Bangkok Bombay
Calcutta Cape Town Dar es Salaam Delhi
Florence Hong Kong Istanbul Karachi
Kuala Lumpur Madras Madrid Melbourne
Mexico City Nairobi Paris Singapore
Taipei Tokyo Toronto

and associated companies in
Berlin Ibadan

Oxford is a trade mark of Oxford University Press

Printed in Great Britain by
St Edmundsbury Press Limited, Bury St Edmunds, Suffolk

Illustrations by Toni Goffe

Photograph of Sylvia Moody © Don Fagg

Chapter 1

It was Saturday morning in Church Lane and, as usual, all was quiet.

There were only ten houses in Church Lane. Most of the people who lived there hated noise. But the Hill family were different. There was Mrs Hill, her son Jack, and her daughter, Kate, and they lived at Number One, Church Lane.

Jack was ten and Kate was nine. Everyone agreed that the two of them made more noise than the rest of the street put together.

The neighbours were always complaining about it.

'I'm sorry,' Mrs Hill would say, 'I do try to keep them quiet. But they are children, you know. They need to let off steam a bit.'

Mrs Hill had lodgers. At the moment, Carla was staying with them. Carla was Italian and she was studying English. She was nice and she sometimes looked after Jack and Kate. But Carla couldn't keep them quiet either.

'Children,' she would beg, '*bambini*, pleeese to stop making too much noise!'

And Jack and Kate would giggle about
Carla's English and be quiet for a bit.
But soon they would forget and start
running about and shouting again.

'Oh, oh, oh,' Carla would groan.
'Such noisy *bambini*!'

On this particular Saturday afternoon, Mrs Hill had to go shopping.

'Jack, Kate,' she said, 'I've got to go shopping this afternoon. I'm leaving you with Carla and I want you to promise that you'll be quiet and behave yourselves. I'll be back at five o'clock. Will you be all right?'

'Of course, Mum,' said Jack. 'What can happen to us here? Nothing ever happens in Church Lane.'

'It's not like on TV, Mum,' said Kate.
'Children on TV have adventures. They
fight lions and things like that. But
nothing happens to us!'

'Well, I'm sorry,' said her mother,
'but we don't have lions in Church
Lane. You'll have to find something else
to do.'

She put on her coat.

'Now, be good!' she said. 'Carla will
make you some tea. Why don't you
read a book or play a game? But please
– don't make a noise. I don't want you
upsetting Elsie or Donald.'

She gave the two children a hug and went out.

'Elsie and Donald – ugh!' said Kate when her mother had gone. 'I'd rather meet a lion any day than them – they really scare me.'

'They scare everyone in Church Lane!' her brother said.

Elsie and Donald were their neighbours at Number Three, Church Lane. They lived very quietly with their two cats. Every day, they and their two cats sat by the window watching. They knew everyone in the road. They saw everything that happened.

But today nothing was happening in Church Lane. The road was completely quiet.

Chapter 2

'So,' said Jack, 'what shall we do this afternoon? Carla, will you play a game with us?'

'Later,' Carla said. 'I prepare some food now. What you want for tea?'

'Egg and chips,' said Jack.

'No, fish fingers,' shouted Kate.

At once the two children started arguing. But Carla could shout even louder than them.

'*Silenzio!*' she screamed. '*Silenzio!* I make you egg and chips *and* fish fingers. Please to make ready the table.'

'She means "set" the table,' Jack said.

'No, she means "lay" the table,' said Kate.

Carla's voice thundered out of the kitchen. '*Silenzio!*'

At that moment the doorbell rang.

'So!' said Carla, coming into the hall. 'Now Elsie and Donald come to complain about too much noise!'

She opened the front door. A tall woman wearing a black coat and carrying a large black bag was standing outside.

'Oh, good afternoon,' she said. 'I'm collecting for our next jumble sale. Have you any old clothes or books that you could give me?'

Carla hesitated.

'A moment, please,' she said.

She called Jack and Kate into the hall.

'*Bambini*,' she said, 'this lady wants books for a jumble sale. Can you give some you no read any more?'

The children nodded and ran upstairs to the playroom where they kept all their books.

Carla waited in the hall talking to the woman. But after a few moments there came the sounds of a loud argument from upstairs.

'I'm giving this one,' Kate was shouting.

'No, I want that. We'll give this one,' Jack yelled back. There were thumps and shrieks and the sound of books crashing on the floor.

'*Mamma mia!*' exclaimed Carla.
'Those children! Excuse please.'

She ran upstairs and found Jack and
Kate struggling together in the middle
of a pile of books.

She pulled them apart.

'One book each,' she said. 'Now!
Finish!'

Jack and Kate went silent and sulky.
They each picked up a book and
followed Carla back downstairs.

But when they got down to the hall,
the woman was gone.

'There,' said Carla, 'she have no
patience with your fighting.'

She went out to the front gate and saw
the woman walking quickly away down
the road.

'Hallo,' she shouted. 'We have books!'

But the woman didn't answer. She
didn't even turn round.

'She has took it,' gasped Carla, whose English got even worse when she was upset. 'That woman – she has took the clock. Quick, I must telephone the police.' She ran to the telephone and dialled 999.

A woman answered.

Fire, police or ambulance?

Police!!

Address?

One, Church Lane

And why do you want the police?

Carla went back to the house. Just as she reached the door she was almost knocked over by Jack and Kate who were rushing out to find her.

'Carla,' Jack wailed, 'the clock's gone.'

'What you mean?' Carla asked.

'The clock,' said Kate. 'The clock in the hall – it's gone.'

Carla looked rou... true: the antique ... hall table was n...

'There is thief in the road,' Carla
shouted. 'She has took our clock.
Please hurry and you can catch her.'

'All right,' said the woman. 'Keep
calm. The police are on their way.'

Carla banged down the telephone.

'Police come,' she said to the children
who were standing in the hall and
watching with wide-open eyes. 'You
two stay here.'

And with that Carla ran out into the road. She could still see the woman in the distance.

'Stop!' she yelled, and began to run down the street. 'Stop, thief!'

The net curtains of Number Three, Church Lane gave a big twitch as Elsie and Donald peered out to see what was happening.

Chapter 3

'What is it, Donald?' Elsie asked.
'What's all the noise about?'

'It's those Hills again,' Donald said.
'It's that student of theirs. She's dancing
about in the road and shrieking.'

At that moment a police car came
roaring into Church Lane and
screeched to a stop outside Number
One. Its siren was wailing loudly.

Two police officers jumped out of the car and began running down the road after Carla and the woman.

'Stop!' they yelled. 'Stop! Police!'

People came running out of all the other houses in Church Lane.

'What is it?' they called to each other. 'What's going on?'

Jack and Kate were still standing in the hall at Number One. They could hear all the shouting and yelling in the street. They wanted to see what was happening.

'Come on,' said Jack. 'Let's go out and look.' He stepped out of the front door.

'No,' said Kate. She grabbed hold of him. 'Come back. Carla told us to stay here.'

'Let go!' shouted Jack, trying to pull himself free of Kate.

'You let go!' Kate yelled, and the two children struggled in the doorway.

Kate hung on to the door with one hand and on to Jack with the other. But Jack was too strong for her. He pulled her out over the step and the door banged shut behind her.

At that moment Carla appeared at
the gate with one of the police officers.
She was holding the antique clock.

'It's all right,' she told the children.
'We catch the thief. We get the time
back.'

Jack and Kate ran out to the gate.
They saw the other police officer sitting
in the car with the woman in black.

The neighbours were gathering
round talking excitedly.

'We've never had the police in
Church Lane before,' they said. 'What a
commotion!'

'I'll have to come in and ask you a few questions,' the first police officer said to Carla.

But at that moment his radio began to crackle. He listened for a moment and then said, 'Sorry, emergency – there's an accident on the ring road. We'll have to go now – I'll come back later.'

He leapt into the car and drove off at top speed. The wail of the car's siren was soon lost in the distance. Silence fell again on Church Lane.

The neighbours began to go back to their houses. The net curtains at Number Three stopped twitching.

'Come now, please, children,' Carla said. 'Too much excitement! Let's go in and have the tea.'

She led the way up the steps to the front door.

'Who shut the door?' she asked. She gave it a push but it wouldn't open.

'Is locked!' she announced. 'Who did this?'

'It was Kate,' said Jack. 'She pulled it.'

'I didn't – it was Jack. He pulled me,' said Kate.

'*Silenzio!*' said Carla. 'See what you have done. Now we are in street!'

Crossly she thrust the clock into Jack's hands and began to walk round the house trying all the doors and windows. They were all locked.

'So,' she said, 'we sit here with clock and wait your mother. Fantastic!'

Chapter 4

'My bedroom window's open,' Kate
said. 'We could climb in that way.'

They all looked up. It was true.
Kate's bedroom window was open and
there was a wide drainpipe running up
the side of the house very close to it.

Carla sighed. 'When I come here,'
she said, 'no-one tell me my job is
climbing. Now stay here, please, and
keep the clock.'

Carla climbed carefully up the pipe
while the two children watched,
holding their breath.

'You're nearly there, Carla,' Jack called.

'Be careful, Carla,' Kate shouted.

'*Silenzio!*' yelled Carla.

She had got up to the level of the
window. She reached out to grasp the
frame when suddenly there was a loud
noise:

DONG!

Jack gave a yelp of surprise. He had forgotten the clock he was holding.

DONG!

The antique clock was striking four!

DONG! DONG!

The sudden noise startled Carla. She lost her foothold on the pipe and came slithering down to the ground. She landed with a crash and began to wail. 'Oh, oh, my leg. I break my ankle. Help!'

The children were shocked. For a
minute they didn't know what to do.

Then Jack said, 'You stay with Carla.
I'll phone 999 – just like Mum told us
to do in an emergency.'

'Phone from where?' Kate said.

'From Elsie and Donald's,' said Jack
bravely.

He ran round to Number Three and
hammered on the door.

The net curtain twitched and Elsie
and Donald peered out at him.

'Help!' Jack shouted. 'Help! We need an ambulance. Quick!'

Elsie came to the front door and opened it.

'What is it now?' she asked. 'First it's that Italian girl shouting and yelling up and down the road. Then it's the police. Then it's clocks chiming and people shrieking in the front garden. Now what's wrong?'

'Sorry,' said Jack, 'I've got to phone for an ambulance. Emergency.'

He saw the telephone in the hall and he ran straight past her. Elsie just stared at him. Jack picked up the receiver and called 999.

The same woman answered.

Fire, police or ambulance?

Ambulance!

Address?

One, Church Lane

Again? You've just called the police...

'I know,' said Jack. 'But now we need
an ambulance. Carla has hurt her
ankle. Please hurry!'

'All right,' the woman said. 'Keep
calm! The ambulance is on its way!'

Jack put the phone down and ran back
to Carla and Kate. Elsie and Donald
followed him outside.

'What next?' they said to each other.
'What next?'

A few moments later an ambulance came tearing into Church Lane. Its siren was wailing loudly. It screeched to a stop outside Number One and two ambulance men jumped out.

The neighbours all came running out of their houses again.

'What's happening now at Number One?' they asked.

The ambulance men ran over to
Carla and began to examine her.

'You're all right,' one of them said.
'Nothing broken. You've just had a
nasty shock.'

He went back to the ambulance and
stopped the siren. Once again peace
fell in Church Lane.

Chapter 5

Elsie and Donald, who had been
standing with their hands over their
ears, went back into Number Three. The
rest of the neighbours went back to
their houses muttering to one another.
'An ambulance in Church Lane!' they
said. 'That's never happened before!'

The second ambulance man helped
Carla to her feet.

'You'll soon be all right,' he told her.
'Just go inside and rest a bit.'

Carla gave a little sob.

'We can't get inside,' Kate explained to the man. And she began to tell him how they came to be locked out.

But just at that moment there was an ear-splitting noise from inside the house. It was louder than the noise of a hundred clocks.

'Oh, oh,' said Carla. She grabbed hold of the ambulance man and cried, 'The fire alarm. The chips!'

'What?' asked the man.

'It's our tea,' cried Kate. She and Jack rushed to the kitchen window and looked inside. The kitchen was full of smoke.

'The chip pan!' yelled Jack. 'It's on fire!'

Carla was clinging on to the ambulance man and shouting hysterically.

'I burn up house,' she screamed. 'Mrs Hill no happy.'

The ambulance man bellowed at her to be quiet. Then he took a phone from his pocket and called 999.

The same woman answered again.

Fire, police or ambulance?

Fire brigade please

Address?

One, Church Lane

One Church ... look here, is this some sort of joke?

A joke?

'Well, first you called the police, then the ambulance. Now you want the fire brigade,' said the woman crossly.

'Yes, we do!' the man said. 'And quick! A house is on fire.'

'All right, all right,' said the woman. 'Keep calm. The fire engine is on its way. But please – don't call again!'

In a few moments the fire engine came thundering into Church Lane.

Its siren was wailing loudly. It juddered to a stop outside Number One and a small army of firemen jumped out.

'Where's the fire?' they shouted.

'In the kitchen,' Jack told them. 'But we're locked out.'

The firemen quickly put a ladder up to the bedroom window and one of them climbed in with a fire extinguisher.

All the neighbours were pouring out of their houses again. They ran down the road to Number One.

'A fire!' they shouted. 'Number One is on fire!'

Suddenly the smoke alarm stopped. Then the fireman opened the front door from the inside. He was holding a very black chip pan.

'You can say goodbye to your tea,'
he said, 'but the kitchen is all right.
You can go inside now. You were lucky
it wasn't worse.'

Without a word Carla and the two
children trooped inside the house. Jack
put the clock down on the hall table.

Outside the neighbours were
returning to their houses again. They
were in shock.

'It's too much for one day,' they said.
'We can't take any more!'

The ambulance men returned to their van and drove off, and the firemen climbed back on the fire engine and drove away too.

The sound of the sirens faded away into the distance and an unnatural calm settled on Church Lane.

Elsie and Donald were still by their window.

'Donald,' Elsie said, 'Draw the curtains, please. I never want to see anything in Church Lane ever again!'

At Number One Carla and the two children were waiting for Mrs Hill to come back.

After a while, Jack said, 'Sorry, Carla!'

'Sorry, Carla,' Kate echoed him.

'You sorry, I sorry!' Carla told them.

Then they sat quietly until Mrs Hill came home.

She was back at five.

'Hello, everyone,' she said cheerfully as she came in through the door. 'You look a bit gloomy. Have you had a nice quiet afternoon?'

About the author

I am a writer and translator of children's books and I also work with children and adults who find reading difficult.

I was born in Yorkshire and after college, I went to work in Greece for fifteen years. I lived in a little castle on the Island of Crete where there were three enormous dogs.

Now I live in London in a very quiet street and that is what gave me the idea for this story...

Other books at Stages 12, 13, and 14 include:

Billy's Luck by Paul Shipton
Cool Clive by Michaela Morgan
Front Page Story by Roger Stevens
Pet Squad by Paul Shipton
Sing for your Supper by Nick Warburton

Also available in packs
Stages 12/13/14 pack   0 19 916879 2
Stages 12/13/14 class pack   0 19 916880 6